The Place That We Keep After Leaving

After Leaving

John B. Lee

Black Moss Press

2008

Library and Archives Canada Cataloguing in Publication

Lee, John B., 1951-
  The place that we keep after leaving / John B. Lee.

Poems.
ISBN 978-0-88753-444-7

  I. Title.

PS8573.E348P53 2008   C811'.54   C2008-901704-8

Cover Image: Landis Doyle

The 64/10 series is published by Black Moss Press at 2450 Byng
Road, Windsor, Ontario N8W 3E8. Black Moss book are distributed
by LitDistco. All orders should be directed there. Or write to www.
blackmosspress.com.

Black Moss Press would like to acknowledge the generous support of
the Canada Council and the Ontario Arts Council for their publishing
programs.

The Canada Council | Le Conseil des Arts
for the Arts | du Canada

ONTARIO ARTS COUNCIL
CONSEIL DES ARTS DE L'ONTARIO

ACKNOWLEDGEMENTS

"Head Lifted, I look at the Moon" from a line by Li Po

Poems from The Place That We Keep After Leaving have appeared in Feast of Equinox, Hammered Out, The Ambassador, Myth Weavers, Voices Israel, and selection of the poems were shortlisted for the OrisonéSouwesto writing award. This work received a Writers Reserve Grant from The Ontario Arts Council under the working title Catching Blue Frogs in the Somerset Swamp.

Black Moss Press would like to thank the talented editorial and publishing teams involved in the production of this book. Their labour has been invaluable in every respect. These include: Eric Agnolin, Meighen D'Angelo, Kendel Doyle, Samina Esha, Kirsten Goodacre, Laura Hall, Kate Hargreaves, Hannah Larking, Tara Oades, Crystal Patterson, Janina Rosonke, Kacy Sawchuk, Melissa Shnarr-Rice, Caitlin Shaw, and Emily Wunder.

for Cathy who loves the lake

WHAT RHYMES WITH DUCK

I was sitting on the dock
fishing with my son
casting for invisibility
where nibbles prove the water
occupied
and we were watching
a solitary drake
slowly circling
propelling itself with webbed feet
compassing a wet yard
and waddling his feathered tail
much like a tethered ship
of hollow bones and little wings
his plimsol line
but the lazy float of shallow thought
and "do ducks know
they're ducks?" my son asks
"or dogs dogs," I say
to put him off ...

consider then
the cloven egg
hermetic as a wobbling rock
the wind beyond its shell
perhaps it contemplates
the colour white
the lime-washed stone
the polished pebble
and the moon

CATCHING BLUE FROGS

the eight-year-old boy, Noah Jukes
who caught
a blue bullfrog
said of himself
"I've been doing this
for years"
as if in the backdrift
of time
in time before memory time
waiting in the ponds
of Somerset swamp
he'd been lingering unborn
in the pre-dawn mists
of antediluvian spring
also in the post-dusk haze
milk-brushed like a chalk-dusted black
where the singular song
of amphibious night
was writing
the fog of the soul
in the voice of the water
pollywog strong
with its spermy tadpole throb
where one axanthic
and therefore blue event
hopped to be caught
in the mind
like a living fragment
of heaven
a blinking singing four-toed wonderful

sky-tattered remnant
of morning—
science says—
"take away yellow
and frogs become blue"
a one in a million
lack-gene rarity

waiting for boys
with light in their hands

THE DOG LIES DOWN IN THE WATER

the dog lies down
in the lake
then rolls in the sand

so there he stands
like a sugar-dusted cake

a brick
for building a one-dog wall

and he will soon enough
rattle it all away
as dogs do

rolling their ribs
like barrels come loose on a deck

and doing
the work of dogs
accomplishing nothing
but splash and scatter

and the lively
chaos of love

WATER WILL FIND A WAY

all day it rained
then water came rushing
down the hill in torrents
seeking the lake, sculpting a shallow
gully in soft sand collapsing inward
to the left of the footbridge
and it washed
at the roots of a leaning locust
the one I'd come to love
casting its shade at a cant
on the thereby blackened beach
tracking the sun in the day and the moon in the night
and then with a slow
subsidence of earth
the rootwork gave in the ground
and the locust sighed down
like a thin man dying
so it set itself
leaf and thorn
on the fence rail
balanced on twig tip
and feather green branch
as it is with hover and float
as it is
with the dignity and balance
of sacred stone
impossible to behold
the Archimedes lever and fulcrum

that lifts the soul
makes light the gravity
of loss

some say it's better gone
it spoiled the view

I say to them, "my friends,
it was the view!"
and gone or not
it stays in lofts of going
its roots
like bones in graves.

CLOSING CRANK-OUT WINDOWS
IN THE RAIN

this morning in your nightgown out of doors
closing windows in the rain, I saw you
in the farouche flurry
of wild shy weather, white wet
cotton clung like a flowing
to your shape
of the luminous motion of mist
your hem floating
to the very let out of the vapouring light
and the light
came sighing down your body
in a limpid caress
like the impossible hands of my soul.

PAUSING TO CONSIDER ONE SOLITARY SUMMER ORCHID

he held the single bloom on its delicate stem
lifted to the light
by the gently turning reverence
of his hand
like a fairy slipper
lost in flight
into the wild green grass
waving farewell to the world

and there it was
mere weed orchid on the ditch lip
where mud was scooped in a curve
by the shovel face of careful men
sculpting a way for trail water
and run off gone dry

"I don't show this to everyone"
he says
of the delicate yellow
prayer line of late spring lifted like a lost girl's glove
in his palm

does it not fade to be touched
by the light
does it not fail
in the leaf to be seen
like the fear of a beautiful child undressing for bed

see how it hides
in the blade sweep
of a breath of warm wind as it passes
even a shadow
might crush as it crosses to darken the bloom
even a voice
might shiver its yellow to fading
like the blowing of water from poolings on paper

and only the thinning of ink
only a trailing to silence
only a sentient quiet
only a slow disappearing
of dream light
can catch it

what vanishes there
in the sleeper's domain
the time that we measure
the place that we keep
after leaving

BAREFOOT ALONG THE SHORE

a woman with shoes in her hands
is walking west
barefoot along the shore
she feels the sand as if
the sift of time
were drifting down
the slender bell glass
of her toes
what intimacy of earth
the lover's dust
as slow caresses of a private promenade

a man is waded to the waist
within the lake
his wet suit
darkened at the water line
he's sunk in circles
gut and wrists
immersed in chill
below the blue umbilicus
a half-complete creation
still for still

and there between
the scribe of shore
and scribe of sky
so straight
it sends the sky to school
I witness how we seem to want
the world within to blend becoming with become

and this
the slow return
of old communions
in a covenant of cloud

the silence
thinks in birdsong
and what is gentle in us
lets it sing

MOST MORNINGS

most mornings
my good neighbour
carries his little daughter
down the steps
to the lake
where they stand
so she might regard with joy
her still reflection
this being for her
a summer
too young to remember

and she rides
her father's rib cage
where their two hearts
brush and touch
like wing tips into water
and this
it seems
is the flight of our souls
this brevity of perfect love
this father
and this child

a kite to keep in a drawer
when the wind
is a withering string

STAY WITH ME

the woman coming lightly down the stairs
says to her bounding forward
and freely disobedient
big dog
"now Sweetie—stay with me"
which he does not!

and he pauses
in our garden
lifting his leg
to drizzle the blanching Hosta
"Don't do that ..." she says
meaning the thing
he's already done
this completely accomplished
crushing act of marking
the blighted leaves
with the toxic urictation
like acid rain

and then
she's off to the sand
where he ranges
out of reach of her voice

as she laughs along
controlling him
as I might control lake swell, apple shade
cloud cover
with the breath of my wishes

this Rotweiller woman
watches
as he squats
and uncoils
from his bowels
the great black-brown mound of himself
abandoned like boat rope
lost on the beach

and she loves
the way he plunges in
among swimmers
laying siege to sand castles
with the great wide
sweep of his happy tail
and all apologies
to children
regretful of their ruined walls

wherever she is
she drags her shadow
like the dark rattle of a broken leash

EVERYWHERE BLUE

I'm alone at the lake
watching the smoothwater
powdersand
beauty of morning
under an everywhere blue
seamline of heaven
with time in its glass
like heartdrift
and a lone gull floating
the shore

last evening
a man told me
of the folly-a-deux
of two lovers
who fell into sorrow
with death
like the shadow of sleep
they were dreaming
they were sudden as stones in a bed
and were gone from their breasts
without breath

as into my world
there came walking
a woman with daughters
lifting their hems
as they waded
and laughing along
clutching their cloth
to keep their skirts dry
and what is the flower's illusion
of summer to them
what white reflection
of lotus and light
how weightless is joy
to these girls
who cry to their mother
and race
among splashes
like dancers who sink in the shattering floor

all buoyant and luminous
colour
all radiant darkness
on sand
we are twinned
by the sun on the water
we are doubled
by shade on the earth.

IN THE SHINING WAY

this is perhaps the last summer
these girls will allow
their father
this innocent privilege
to touch
their naked bodies
on the beach
to stand them
in the shining way
polishing their brown bottoms
like waxed apples
patting dry their thighs
before moonlight
pulls forth its first red ribbon
daubing their
damp bellies like washed peaches
to him they are precious
perfect
and entirely lovely
as they wriggle and laugh
and break away
from his careful embraces
lifting their beautiful bodies
as like the lonesome
levitation
of evaporate angels
the gulls take flight
where they run

their mother
comes chasing
and clucking her tongue
with empty little swimsuits
draping her wrists
for she knows
that in time
they will learn
how the fallen
will see them
and they'll shadow their shame
with fanning hands

THE ART OF FAILURE

today
I watch
a father and his son, out
playing catch
upon the beach
and I'm amazed
at the variety of ways
they manage
to miss their mutual throws
the father wears an older mitt
sweat-watered brown
the son
a long-leathered deep pocket glove
the black palm well-padded
they stand, incompetent for all
at thirty paces apart
the ball goes wobbling high, or wiffling wide
or plopping short
or tipping off a thumb
to plunk in sand

or simply bouncing from the stitch
to drop straight down and landing
at the feet
much like an orchard's
windfalls or a poison eater's
peach
a sleeper's apple
or a wormy plum
the father mentors
and the son responds
but neither learn
the man admired by his lad
is worse
and worse than that
he does not know how bad
he is because he's awful bad
beyond the know of bad

WHAT PREVAILS

one gull
who cannot hold the ground
blows sideways on the sand
for want of weight
his feathers
disarranging backwards
to the lee
much like a sat on hat
or crush of wings
until he turns
beak forward
to the weather's breath
that grooms and preens
and smoothes his pins
to prove his tail a stillness
worth the work
the wind
that's cowlick wild
unstraitens weeds
and times the foam of things
is in this word-whipped world
a friend of one direction
and a foe of four

all fellow flights
come wheeling to the beach
umbrellas loft
their drifting shades
and stamp the deck
like anger in the ram

and that lone gull
keeps trying
with a weakening will

THE FOG ON THE LAKE OF MORNING

the fog
blurs water and sky
and is grey
like wet paper dipped, lifted and hung to dry
we lose the far island
cannot see the dark tree line
the ragged shade rub of a lead-edged wood
gone like the slow sinking away
of a broken ship all-hands drowned
in the doomed distance of Pottahawk
cannot see
the sand horizon of Long Point
in the milky cataract
of this ambergris weather
like the sad failure of old eyes aging
the lighthouse wisdom
of invisible things
into which the gulls
bloom like blown-full lilies
carried by drift
and the string clutch
of such gravities

as return them
as children might pull
balloons in
from where they are
angels of big blue breath
and the translucent exhale
of adult wishes

these are the burned
and burning
clarities of this very hour

the way
a dream moth
reifies itself in fluttering
sleep of a waking mind
ringing the velvety cloche
of its wings
on the late-to-die porch globe glowing

what this poem requires
of us, dear reader
of me with my Dixon HB
and you
and your future malingering
receiving this code
in the lonesome surrender
of moments
between us
is locked in the dawdle
and pauses
the lines of this language

like burying linen
to gather
the earth that it carries
or letting
the weave take the river
the soak
of a fluvial surface and silting
wretted by float till it gathers
its flaws
like the tugging of buttons
with movement from breathing
the heaven it holds
over autumn
its anthem, the talking of geese
in their compassing chevrons

what's the world
in the wind whip of tresses
what's the sky
to the wading of hearts
when we're wet
to the watches from falling

EVERYTHING WITHIN US

one August morning
the sand spits surfaced
in the shallows of my homely lake
like the several islands
of a drowned man's belly
and we thought then
of the dog day
low tides
in the diurnal heat
of mid summer
with memory of night breath
cool in the flesh
like alcohol in cloth
to draw the fever from the heart
falling off into darkness
like a broken-stem rose
where a woman
might carry an inclosing of love

and I watched the same moon
and such similar stars
only lost evenings ago
in the country chateau
in now distant Bourgogne
watching heaven
heave its breast
with a buxom inhale
at the open window above the bed on the farm
those galaxies of Charlemagne
and the blue belief of kings
in the wheat crop of that foreign sky

and thus
the water comes
to comfort us with awe

the grey relief of too much human light
the artificial shadow of a leaning shade

and everything within us
a silkening of soul
like clarifying oil on curves of glass.

THE TREE OF BEAUTIFUL DANGERS

what broken-winged angels are we
at rest in lost boughs
in the tree of beautiful danger
as children we longed
to climb there cracking the grafts
to where greyness thins out of reach
beyond the gravity of apples
to feel aflutter or fall from season
like fledged sparrows
to find grief
in blue fear
far past the flicker of tall fruit
where it clings
to its last brief softening
so unforseen autumn
hangs on into winter as its stem stops over-wound time.

well, there we went
singing into the dizzy designs
arriving at shade fathoms of deepening green
in the loss-measured light
seeking flush in the quivering leaf
with a silence
a satiate awe
a quality of drift
that feathers the instep
and lifts as weightlessness lifts
a water stain dimming warm sand

for what thickens our quiet
colours our watch

who rattles a ladder then
shortens heaven
lowers the largening moon.

EVEN THIS TREE LIKE A LONESOME WOMAN

even the tree
like a lonesome woman
requires the blushing of beautiful light
look to love from the rumouring moon
fallen to blossomed faded lawns
from a perfumed buzzing gone still
in the heart and the heat of the bloom
oh, apple-breasted
peach buxom
pear bottomed dawn
what I once saw
gave the orchard its autumn
the morning its moth
but the hive
is a ghost house
that hums in the wind
like the whisper of paper in rain
and it hangs
like a lantern glown dark
on a fluttering wick
and the word without wings
is a honey that stales
in the comb

I am watching
it whiten the jar
all the wax-crowned perfection
of home
all the aspic and alum
won't winter this death
with the garden gone quiet
the meadow becalmed
when the bee-keeper's smoke drops no drone
we are lost in a casual glare
with our hands
to a sting or an itch or a burn or a bite
we are lousy with life
without hope.

THE VANISHING

I

the island
vanishes
the point is lost
the tree line
blurs like thumb smudge
and is gone
the lighthouse
on the sandspit
can't be seen
though it has left its rumour
in remember
like a planet
or a star
and we know it's there
out past
the work of gulls
the harbour calls
to shore

II

the body
is piano boned
it thrums
below the sympathetic rhythms
of the house
we walk at night, we are become
the lonesome
metronome
clock pendulous
in us
falls deep much like the level dark
in failing wells

we plunge
past empty thirst
to find
the source of dream

III

I plucked a wrecked gull
dying from the beach
and carried
him by delicate feather force
of wing tip where I felt
life drift away by tickles in the quill
almost become a fluttering of stone

and yet I flung him
where he fell and failed to fly
through shadows of himself
to where
the heaviness of heaven's blue
became a pushing down of day

he was too weak to lift that
veil-weight with a final sigh
poor thing
he pecked the earth
and swallowed hard

his nostrils carved the sand

IN THE SOLEMN RHYTHMS

"the Sufi master recognizes her and loves her in the ruins of desert
encampments, in the solemn rhythms of the magnificent swaying of camels ..."
Maurice Glaton on the poems of Iba Arabi, 1165-1240

this morning I watch
a young woman
disrobe on the sand
she loosens her skirt
and lets it fall to the earth
so it drifts
like a circle of shade
and she wades
to her thighs
in the chill
where she rattles her hands

and here too
I see in the foreground
an old tree-trunk suckered with russets
the weed thin refusal to die
of three frail sand branches
spindling out of the stump
of what we lost last summer
to cruel weather
and the awful aftermath of wind
and smoking saws
it has rotted away with the winter
to the empty O of its dust
seeded with twitch

SOMETIMES THE WAY OF WEEDS

our dog
used to lie on the floor
and chew
at the balled up fur
of her tail
where it was tangled
in cocklebur
like bad mending
and she'd nip them
singly from her tufted paws
and set them out
beside her on the rug
grown soggy with saliva
those prickly burdock seeds
brought home from ditch
and fallow field
as if she were their wind

and yesterday
my wife and I
went about uprooting from the beach
the sandbur
with its spiny pericarps
like pins in wool
they clung to us for love
our socks
were jeweled with painful green
our sleeves
came cuffed in swarms
of glassy grass
that nipped the wrist
and bit the pulse
and needled up the arm
and stung the flesh
like anger in the hive

they found the belly
found the breast
they feathered in the hair
and fell away like honey makers full of smoke
each plant we plucked
barbed backwards from its roots
and sprung like wire snipped in war
the kind might cut a man
in half

we bagged the weed
tamped it down with shovel steel
and went about the business
of nursing danger
from our prickly socks
our beetled shirts
be-scarabbed like a desert corpse
oh we were careful
as any fear-filled Androcles
until we had them all

that night in dream
my wife awoke
startled by
a thing we'd brought to bed
for memory a little shadow
in her cotton gown
too real to be untrue
the dog mouth of the dark
had left its burr
the plant had found
its wind.

BUILDING SOMETHING GREEN

I am watching the tractor man
travel back and forth
along the tourist beach
with his bucketful
of water weed
carted away
to where he is building
something green
something sand-worthy
from the toothless
and endlessly ruminant
moon-sorrowing surf
churning its cud and bolus
like a wet-mouthed cow

and I am reminded
of summers and summers ago
in an uncommon warm
how algae gathered
in the black-soup shallows
where we waded to the waist
in the stinking still
as in a manure lagoon
and we worked our forks
among wriggling red worms
and the thickening spoor
that clung to the tines
like swatches of cloth
torn from the putrefied shirts
of the drowned

and we heaped it
like hay to dry

oh what a stagnant applause
we heard
when only boat churn
set an undulous surface
swell in motion
slapping the sand
like the dying in oil of a duck

and then
after weeks and weeks
of futile working in crews
that grew to dozens
parenthetic of opinions
of what to do what to do
while the minnow-man
laughed through his nets

then with one night of storm
it was gone

the same lake
swallows five fathers
and several sons
at a gulp
then grinds at their ghosts
and spits up their bodies
like pits

when mud comes clear
in a man

like the two-eyed dust
of being alive

what swims into view
from within

like the touch-bottom thought
of a saturate awe

how we silt into separate
selves

ah me, with my breath
in this ink
and you
with your thumb
in a book

I've my hands
on a fork full of wind

and I'm filling the sky
with new stars

HEAD LIFTED, I LOOK AT THE MOON

I

last night
my wife and I stood together
on the street
in the town
outside the local laundromat
extolling
the brilliant blemished white
stone of the moon
as if it were
a unique and irreplaceable
event of briefly borrowed light
where it sat
like a circle of burning frost
too early to outlast
the eternity of now
within the milk-blue sea
of what melts away
becoming heaven
without memory
and mind
and I felt
in that monumental moment
the full round spirit
of Li Po
and I stood
shouting about beauty

as a cyclist spun past
without so much
as looking back
over his shoulder

II

when we got home
we sat
out front
on our cottage step
where we
kept the moon company

holding hands with darkness
courting the starless night

III

the riderless bicycle
leans against a fence

it knows more about the moon
than its rider
who hurried home to rush
indoors at this hour, and is
watching the war
through the false window
of a tv screen

isn't it sad
what we fail to notice

by the dying of strangers
in distant lands
or by the broken ones
who suffer still
or by those of us
who are not there

the moon
lifts the hem of the soul
so it dare not trail
itself through the seas of time
though it touch
the poet's mind
like the pleasant blush of dream

IV

late summer lies
in the path of frost

and the lake
is fogged with thoughts of dawn

the cyclist
falls asleep in the talk show
glow of David Letterman's laughter

and moonlight
keeps itself in veils of sorrow
like a widow's wedding linen
awaiting
the mischief of a curious child

V

Li Po
old friend

transform me
like a worm of God
and let me fly
this chrysalis of words

a thousand years
since when
another thousand years
from now

the future learns
the past

as poets die
into their ink

between stone temples
and the dimpled bones
of man

there is a covenant
of colour

a billion butterflies
at rest
before tomorrow's flight
across the lake
fold up their wings
in true respect
for ancient journeys made
and journeys
yet to come

they've Mexico's in memory
fritillaries of loss
of orange
with oranges yet to gain

THIS PLACE EXACTLY
THIS TIME CALLED NOW

this place
exactly, this time called now
is where and when the earth
receives the leaf

from twig tip
through shadow swell
the loss of shade
comes close
to settle
with a small
self-sized caress
much like a kiss
but oh, the breath
behind
such tender touch of gravity
the web-caught
heart of spring
can't hold
what autumn wants
of wind
and weather weight
as both come spinning down
to grass

I'm at an outdoor table
tossed in fallen stems
and stoma yellowing the wood
those grand old trees
seem much to me like ladies
who unhook their golden bobs
to rub their ears
and rest

while geese
like bath toys ride the lake
and squawk about
the journey yet to come

I'm north of that
among the gulls
meanwhile the maple
paints my handback ring to wrist
with lightest splash of sugared red

the world is in
a loving mood
although it whispers winter
with a distant wing

SOMEWHERE BETWEEN THESE TWO

sometime during the war
the Nazis passed a law
against the keeping of pets
by Jews

and I'm reading this
in an hour
of assassinated silence
with the weed whipper
lashing hill grass
from where it grows in tussocks
above the lake

and the sun
is bluing the water
where children wade
in radiant haloes
of step waves stirred by walking
their floaters out and away
to where heaven paints a lighthouse
and dock-buoys guard the beach

meantime
a woman scars the recently harrowed sand
with dog-on-leash
and is she on her way
to surrender
the thing she strolls by sniffs and pauses
will she not
walk an empty circle home
or drag her line
like the weight of love as loss

the man descending the outdoor stairs
who stops
to free a forepaw
from the lead
his carefilled gesture
says 'farewell at last, you're lost'

what budgerigar
there were
become green songs of morning
locked in quiet shadows
of a kitchen clock
and sixty million gongs

I'm on the lack-cat lawn
with vacant lap
the weeping child I was
dog-frozen years ago
when joy went winter stiff
to find him in the barn, and dead ...

what world is this
I wonder
that steals us to such pain

I disbelieve in war
my heart drops singing
past the plunge of grief
and mines the mind
my yellow wings
flare up like fire
from the shoulders of an immolated saint
I am all faiths
encaged by burning bones
my last consuming sin
is hope.

LOST

God do me this little favour
I want
women in wind-whipped dresses
clutching cloth
in wild weather
doing that big-shadowed
parachute float
of the hem where the cliff flirts
with glassy crashes of shattering water
and the moon-tugged
foam of the sea sucks backward
from blackness

I want rain
on the raspberries
cows
weeping milk for the barn
and the hay smells
of seven summers
bringing the broken-string bale
dropped through the mow hole
like large flaked fruit of the loft
falling
so it strikes
with a huff of dust
like a hand clap
on an old chesterfield
in an abandoned parlour
where farm-ghosts decide upon standing

and when the cottage bed goes boggy
as uncooked cake

and we two sleepers
sink away
from the ceiling
like slow deflation
of come-clear darkness

I think of my life
as the far west corner subsidence
of a century house
just that much
deeper into the earth
just that much farther from heaven
joisted in muck
like a heavy boat
set in green water
I'll buoy what I've been
and love the burden
with my sky-smudged windows

thrown open
on turmoil
and swirling
the light shafts doing that dust dance
called

the luminous spirit of absence

THE MAN WHO FELL BEFORE THE TREE

the man leaned back
lost ladder
and fell
like a rotten branch breaking its graft
and he broke into old oak along the brittle bone
ant-hollowed
of soul by that last lost grip
and the long surprise
suddenly becoming the treeless
gravity of snap
an earth-loved
autumn crop of lonesome wine sap
gathers to do
all widow-woeful stillness
huffed of life
the door stop barn stone
of the darkened brain
humbled to a meaningless name
the fool skull, the foundation
and the spade-of-amaze
he's also cottage to that

who walks the shovel
to the waterline
accepts his fate as if and when
the man who falls before the tree
fails to
the rope-rattled rungs
and the weather of sway
with an eaves-level feeling
from emptying off the still heights of the heart
like leaf thrill and sparrow song
of touch upon touch

then comes the first pear-sweet dawn
without him
and that thin-shadowed orchard
involves a lazy grooming
where he's dragging the darkness away
with a luminous saw

THE POLAR BEAR DIP AT PORT DOVER

they have come to do
and we
to watch the doing, this year
the winter lake
was iceless as autumn
the water
foaming at the soles of our sensible shoes
like madness and desire in the tide
an indecisive greylit
shallowing of time
as cold as cottage satin lying unattended
luffing in a lonesome bedroom in an all-shuttered dark

and we, the crowd
were waiting by the breakers in our parkas
and our moth-ball scented wools, our toques
and mittens, scarves and mufflers tucked and blowing
when they came running
fleshed in rayon mostly naked but for t-shirts
quilted track pants and knee-length swim suits on the adolescent
boys
racing past the splashline of the wave-shattering shores

going out into the hypothermic will
of what it is
we sometimes try
when things are barely deep enough to notice
rising past ankles and falling like loosened socks
caressing the red alarm of goose-fleshed thighs
and slap-bellied torsos and the fat-bounce of floating bosoms
touching the surface and cork-bobbing like gum-drop candy
spilled from penny bags

men in carried lawn chairs
sit down
the shrinking lads
flapping their flightless arms like doomed auks and ugly angels
some with their ass cracks showing
feeling the humbling sophomoric drag
of the wave force pranking at their trousers

the women shine
and drop themselves into the water
like orchards shaken in a lazy-weathered wind
they rise again and drip and quiver
and giggle and titter and laugh
embracing bracing shivers of themselves
like company come to call
one fellow sits and lingers
up to his heart-line
he wears
a steer-horn hat
ridiculous enough to be loved
he's lard-white
and like a cartoon Viking
waiting to be photographed
and all at once and every one
they come ashore anew
bedraggled by the dampened sloven like those shipwrecked
from the turning of the year

and this their first accomplishment
the coffee brags
the beer stein boasts
the tea steam breaks the silence
with a blustering breath befogged

and yet
old glaciers continue to calve
and vanish
into grey-white waters

TO FEEL THE PULL OF THE SKY

she speaks of herself
and the rapture
as if at any moment
she might be taken up
by miraculous
transformation
in the great whirlwind
of the soul
as I have seen
it done
by Lake Erie water spouts
by leaf swirl
by dust motes
gyring in school corners
of the mind
one might call memory
one might call dream

but there she stands
dog heavy
and full of opinions

like us all
she suffers
the bone moral
of mortality

despite this
butterfly madness
of the mouth
her words mothing up
like struck wool

what she wants
is for the dead to be dead
for the living
to be dead
and for me to be   dead
but I am not
finished my sandwich
and the beer is good

though I feel
the pull of the sky
on my hat
it will not have
my head